TRUCKS AND TRUCKING

·······TRUCKS AND TRUCKING

BY RUTH AND MIKE WOLVERTON

To Karelyn, our very special daughter who always prefered trucks to dolls! With all our love
Mike Wolverton

To Karelyn who keeps on trucking love Ruth.

Franklin Watts
New York / London / Toronto / Sydney / 1982
A First Book

Photographs courtesy of
the Kelly Springfield Tire Company: opp. p. 1;
the Ford Motor Company: p. 3;
Fairbanks Weighing Division, Colt Industries: p. 4;
Chevrolet Truck Division: pp. 7, 43;
the Bekins Company: p. 16;
the White Motor Corporation: pp. 19, 20, 23, 24.

Library of Congress Cataloging in Publication Data

Wolverton, Ruth.
Trucks and trucking.

(A First book)
Bibliography: p.
Includes index.
Summary: Discusses various aspects of professional
truck driving, including rigs, trucking laws, life on
the road, and how to become a truck driver. Defines
the CB ten-code and lists trucking AM radio stations.
1. Truck driving—Juvenile literature.
[1. Truck driving]   I. Wolverton, Mike.   II. Title.
TL230.3.W64   388.3′24   82-6967
ISBN 0-531-04468-8   AACR2

CONTENTS

TRUCKS AND TRUCKING

• • • • • • • • • • • *1*

HEADING FOR SAN ANTONE

Doug Carry and Orm Stewart headed south out of the Windy City on I-57 bound for Alamo Town. They were driving a Pete, hauling furniture for Bekins. Orm backed off on the hammer on account of a chicken coop coming up in front of them. He had a frown on his face. Doug wasn't sure if the frown was because Orm didn't like chicken inspectors or if it was because of the ten-thirteen they got on the radio just now telling them they were heading into an ice storm.

Talking the Language of Truckers

If you have ever heard truckers talk you know that they have a language all their own. It's English, but they have so many nicknames for things and so many special phrases that you need a translation to know what they are talking about!

What was happening was that Doug and Orm were delivering a load of furniture from Chicago, Illinois (the Windy City) to San Antonio, Texas (Alamo Town). All cities and towns have special nicknames in trucker's language. "Pete" is short for Peterbilt, the brand name of the tractor they were driving. "Chicken coop" is the nickname for the weight stations along the highways. The

• *1*

"chicken inspector" is the state police officer in charge of weighing trucks at the weight stations. The "hammer" is the accelerator pedal, and "back off on the hammer" means to slow down. A "ten-thirteen" is a weather report.

What Makes a Truck

Orm owns his own "bucket of bolts," meaning the Peterbilt tractor they were driving. A furniture mover, he leased his tractor out to the Bekins Moving Company that owned the trailer he was pulling. The tractor and the trailer together is what truckers call a truck. If you include the CB radio, which they always have in the cab of the tractor, the entire outfit is called a "rig."

Orm's tractor is green with white shark's teeth painted on the grill. He calls it his "Mean Green Machine," and that is the "handle," or nickname, he uses for himself and his rig when he talks to other truckers on his CB radio.

Inside the Big Rig

A Peterbilt tractor is considered by truckers to be the Rolls Royce of tractors. It is built by hand and has a lot of deluxe features. Like all tractors, it is very expensive. Truckers pay as much for their tractors as most people pay for their homes. Of course, you can actually live in most of the big tractors like the Pete. It has a big double bunk, and there is a mini-kitchen right behind the driver and passenger seats.

Sitting in the cab of a tractor is like being in an airplane's cockpit. Tractor cabs are loaded with controls and gauges. There are gauges for the engine oil temperature, manifold pressure gauges, a gauge for each differential, fuel gauges, and water temperature gauges, to name a few. There is even a gauge that tells drivers the weight of the load they are carrying!

Weight Stations and Weighing In

Even with weight gauges, drivers still have to stop at all the state weight stations and have their loads weighed. This is done by driv-

The tractor and trailer together is what
truckers call a truck. If the CB radio is
included, the entire outfit is called a "rig."

Each state must weigh all trucks
that use the highways.

ing their trucks right onto a big scale. Each state must weigh all trucks that use the highways to make sure the trucks and their loads are not too heavy. A truck that is carrying too much weight can tear up the roads and highways. If a load is too heavy the trucker can get a heavy fine. Too many fines can put a trucker out of business.

Different Truckers and Their Problems

Fines for such offenses as carrying too much weight or speeding are not the only problems truckers have. Delays caused by bad weather and poor road conditions often make the difference between success and failure to a trucker.

Truckers also have problems with special kinds of cargo. For example, a "bull hauler," which is a cattle-truck driver, carries a load of live cattle that can shift and bunch up. If this happens, the load becomes uneven and the trucker can lose control of his or her trailer, even with the best road conditions. Beef haulers must also load and unload frightened cattle. These problems can cause expensive delays, which are especially bad for owner-operator truckers who lease out their rigs for an agreed amount of money and who then have to pay their own expenses. Many truckers are owner-operators. If they are smart business people, they can make a lot more money than if they worked for a company and drew a regular salary every week or month. Of course, what the company person does get—a paycheck—is his to keep whereas the owner-operator has to put money aside for maintenance, taxes, paying a second driver, and so on. But a smart trucker with some luck can make enough money, after taxes, to maintain a high standard of living—as good or better than many other professional people.

Truckers who make the most money and take the greatest risks are produce truckers, those that haul perishable food. These are the truckers with "reefers," or refrigerated trailers, hitched onto their tractors. They must maintain the proper temperature in these trailers with gasoline-powered refrigeration units, because if they reach their destination and the cargo is spoiled they have to buy it! If the produce *does* arrive in good shape, but late, the price of the foodstuff might have changed so much that the market that promised to buy the load can't afford it and refuses to take it. These kinds of problems make produce trucking risky.

The steel haulers, who usually drive a flatbed rig, face other kinds of problems. Steel-hauling truckers must spend a lot of time tying and retying their tarps—the heavy canvas or plastic tarpaulins that protect their cargo from water. Since truckers are paid by the mile for hauling, that tarping time is considered just a part of the service. The steel, other heavy metal, or machinery they haul is a safety hazard, too. If the load should come loose during a quick "panic" stop, it would shift forward and crush the tractor cab, driver and all.

Hazardous Loads

The most dangerous loads are not explosives, but liquids and unbalanced loads.

When a tank-trailer rig filled with liquid brakes to a stop, all the liquid in the tank keeps moving forward. Sometimes a tractor-tanker will stop and start up three or four times before coming to a final halt. The liquid load just keeps pushing the truck when it slops forward. Many of the really big tank trailers have baffles, or partitions, built in to keep the liquid in separate compartments. These baffles diminish the forward motion of the liquid so it does not push so hard on the tractor when the truck stops.

Unbalanced loads like swinging beef cause problems, too. The beef—huge carcasses of meat—hangs from hooks attached to the top of the trailer, and when the truck is in motion the beef swings back and forth. The shifting weight can vibrate the trailer so hard that the entire rig will flip over. Truckers say this sometimes happens when they are rounding a curve with a load of beef. All of a sudden the truck just flips over on its side!

"Double Bottoms"

Pulling "double bottoms," or "twins," (two trailers in tandem), which is legal in thirty-seven states, can be dangerous. The back

There are different kinds of trailers for
different kinds of trucking jobs.

trailer can start swaying from side to side if there are high winds or if the driver must turn the wheel sharply in an emergency. Then there is no way to control the rig except to slow down and pray!

Hijackers, Yesterday and Today

Most of us don't think of cigarettes, liquor, television sets, or radios as dangerous cargo. Yet according to truckers, such cargo *is* dangerous. They say that anything valuable that is hard to identify as stolen property attracts hijackers. One big trailer load of any of the items listed above can be worth more than a quarter of a million dollars.

Hijackers today are not as showy as the criminals of the 1920s who would often pull up to a truck on a lonely stretch of highway with machine guns blazing. These days their favorite trick is to jump on the running board of the tractor when the trucker is waiting at a stop light in the industrial section of a city. Usually armed, the hijackers force the trucker to drive to a secluded spot where accomplices unload the cargo.

Truckers who haul valuable cargo usually are given permission to carry a pistol in their truck. They always back their trailer up to a building at night so that the rear cargo doors cannot be opened without moving the truck. However, cargos are sometimes lost in spite of everything the driver does. One trucker recently reported to police in Chicago that he had had to run off hijackers three times in one night. Then, he went to sleep in his cab and woke up the next morning to find the bottom of his trailer cut open and his whole load of color TV sets gone!

Fortunately, hijackings are few and far between. And in spite of all their problems, most truckers will tell you that they wouldn't trade their life of freedom on the open road for any other kind of job.

Hauling Furniture

Truckers like Orm Stewart will tell you, too, why they do the kind of trucking they do. Most movers haul furniture because they like dealing with people.

Orm and Doug had met the Thompsons back in Chicago when they had supervised the loading of the Thompsons' furniture into their trailer. The whole family had been excited about moving to San Antonio, Texas, and getting a new start in life. Except for the clothes in their suitcases, the Thompsons had entrusted all their possessions to Orm and Doug and Orm's green-and-white Peterbilt tractor.

Orm and Doug had to pull into another weight station right after they crossed the Mississippi River into St. Louis, Missouri, and picked up I-44. While the trailer was getting weighed, Orm checked the weather with the state police officer in charge. When they pulled back onto I-44, Orm put the hammer down and grinned at Doug.

"The chicken inspector says we're legal as an eagle for Missouri highways," Orm said. "But the bad news is that we're hitting snow down at the Oklahoma border and it's snow, sleet, and ice all the way to Texas. Sorry about that—this being your first run right out of truck-driving school and all."

"Hey," Doug said, feeling a little thrill of excitement in the pit of his stomach, "that's okay. That's the way us greenhorns learn about trucking. But I sure hope we get to San Antone before that big trucking show down there is over. I'm really looking forward to that."

"What I'm aiming to do," said Orm, "is to get the Thompsons' household goods to them on time so they don't have to spend days in some motel wondering if they'll ever see their things again. And for that we're going to have to organize a convoy and help everybody through that ice storm down in Oklahoma."

"How will you do that?" asked Doug.

"First we get on the CB radio and find out who is heading our way." Orm picked up the CB microphone and pushed the "talk" button. "Breaker one-nine," he announced, "this is the Mean Green Machine. I need a ten-forty-five. Got a copy?"

ORGANIZING TO OVERCOME TROUBLE

Orm got a copy (report) from several other truckers traveling west on I-44 out of St. Louis, Missouri, heading for Oklahoma. His CB radio request for all CBers within range to answer (ten-forty-five) also put him in contact with a trucker's CB base station at a big truck stop a few miles down the road. The truck-stop operator invited Orm and the other truckers to meet at the truck stop to organize a convoy and make plans for battling the bad weather and road conditions ahead.

Truck Stops
When Orm and Doug pulled into the truck stop they found it to be a "trucker village," like the old cowboys' towns at the end of the cattle trail or a sailor's home port. Anything a trucker could need or want was available at this big and elaborate truck stop. It offered a room for the night, a shower, a haircut, a massage, a sauna, color TV sets tuned to several different channels, pinball machines, electronic games, pool tables, and almost as much merchandise as a supermarket. There was everything from shaving gear to authentic Indian jewelry, which Doug noticed was made in Taiwan!

After all, if you are driving a 60-foot (18-m) tractor semi-trailer you can't drive it downtown to do your shopping. So a trucker shops at these truck stops for all his or her day-to-day necessities as well as for gifts and toys to take home to family and friends.

Truck stops have come a long way. Many years ago they were just small way stations where tired and hungry drivers could get a cup of coffee and a good meal while relaxing for a few moments. These were usually roadside restaurants run by a couple or a family and specializing in good food at a very reasonable price. Truckers were often their only customers. Now, many "four-wheelers"—ordinary tourists in passenger cars—patronize the huge and efficient truck stops run by the major oil companies. All the customers get the same fast food. The only difference is that truckers eat in special sections with more waiters and waitresses so that they can get faster service. In these special sections truckers can eat their meals, drink several cups of coffee, talk to other truckers, and be back on the road in half an hour. Truckers may get larger portions of food at a slightly lower price than the general public being served outside the truckers' section.

Truck-stop operators do not make much of their profits from the food and merchandise they sell to truckers or from the rooms and entertainment they provide. Most of their profit comes from the fuel and repair services they provide. It is usual for a trucker to spend between three and five hundred dollars for fuel and maintenance during a single stop! At the pumps and the service bays truck-stop operators concentrate on providing excellent service to truckers. Good service means repeat business. Most big truck stops pump over 1 million gallons (3.8 million l) of fuel into more than 20,000 trucks every month. Service people who work "out front" live by the slogan, "What the trucker wants, the trucker gets."

Trucking Clothes and Trucking Music

Some truckers like to wear modern cowboy attire: lizard boots, jeans, sculptured leather belts with big metal buckles, and plaid shirts. The shirt must be long sleeved, but the sleeves may be rolled up.

Although there are a few exceptions to the truckers' dress code, there are two things that truckers always find at truck stops: plenty of coffee and a juke box with country and western music. Many of the truckers' favorite musical ballads tell about truckers matching wits with state police officers who must enforce the many and often confusing laws that regulate trucking.

Trucking Laws

Each of the fifty states has its own trucking laws. These laws vary to some degree from state to state. What is legal in one state may not be legal in the next state. But the law must be obeyed, so the "smokeys" (truckers' nickname for police officers) always keep their eyes on the "bandits" (police officers' nickname for truckers). It is sometimes difficult for truckers to keep track of the individual state laws and to keep up-to-date on any changes. So bandits watch out for smokeys, hoping they will not get caught with the wrong kind of driver's license or state permit or with too much weight in their trailer. Not all truckers know every state law and regulation, but the more professional ones make it their business to find out.

Nearly all states require a special license for heavy-duty truck drivers. The license is issued by the state in which the driver lives. These licenses are referred to as "Class A," "Class 1," or "Chauffeur's" licenses. But some states require different classes of these licenses, depending on the gross weight of the rig and/or number of axles on the vehicle. One state (Hawaii) requires as many as seven different classes of driver's licenses for a trucker!

Some states limit the number of trailers that can be pulled by one tractor and some don't. Some states limit the maximum length of the tractor-trailer rig and some don't. And the maximum weight that may be carried on each state's highways differs greatly.

By far the most confusing legal problem for truckers, however, is the permit requirements in each state. A truck tractor may be plastered with many license plates in front, and a trailer may have a dozen states' permit numbers written on the rear doors, but the one for the state the trucker happens to be driving through may have just expired. Or perhaps a new regulation in that state now requires a different kind of permit. Some states have agreements with other states to honor one another's license plates. This is called *reciprocity*. But many states have reciprocity agreements with only four or five bordering states and no others.

Within each state there are also regulations about trucks being driven on county roads and on city streets. County and city police watch truckers to make sure they do not violate these local laws.

There was a time when truckers had to abide by federal government regulations also. These regulations, enforced by the Interstate Commerce Commission (ICC), were in effect from the depression days of the 1930s until July of 1980, when the Motor Carrier Act deregulated the entire trucking industry. Under the old federal regulations, only a limited number of trucking firms were allowed to haul goods between states, and the rates that could be charged for hauling were set by the ICC. Today, any number of trucking firms may compete for the business of hauling goods across the country, and the rates are set by the trucking companies themselves. The result has been the creation of many new trucking companies and more jobs for independent non-union truck drivers. Deregulation has also resulted in more vigilance on the part of state and local authorities.

Is it any wonder that truckers often say they wish they could become invisible when the smokeys are out?

Artwork on Trucks

While truckers may wish to be invisible to the police, they like to be noticed by everyone else. Every trucker is proud of his or her truck. Most go to a lot of effort and sometimes a lot of expense to customize their tractors. Many truck stops offer fancy paint jobs and custom geometric designs with decals, pinstriping, and special chrome parts. You name it, and if the trucker wants it he or she can get it! Some truckers put their children's names on the front of their cabs. Some, like Orm Stewart, name their tractors and decorate the cab with artwork accordingly.

Trucking in the Old Days

Truckers have not always had the fancy, efficient, and comfortable machines they have today, or the good roads on which to drive them. Today's trucks, like the one Orm and Doug drive, with its dozens of lights, gauges, and switches; its air conditioning, tape deck, and CB radio, are the result of many years of hard work.

More than a hundred and fifty years ago, during the 1830s, the first self-propelled carriages began to move over rutted dirt roads in England. These first "automobiles" were powered by steam engines, and they often exploded. These steam carriages were effectively put out of business by the 1865 Locomotives on Highways Act passed by the British Parliament under pressure from railroad and horse-drawn carriage interests. The Act reduced permissible speeds to 2 miles (3 km) per hour in cities and 4 miles (6 km) per hour on country roads! Steam engines continued to be used to transport goods on rivers and oceans, but on land the main means of locomotion remained horsepower during the next sixty years.

In 1883 Gottlieb Daimler, a German engineer, invented a high-speed internal combustion engine that could run on petroleum spirits (gasoline). In 1886 he used it in one of the first automobiles ever built. Karl Benz of Germany is also credited with inventing the internal combustion engine. He ran his first car in 1885. This new form of power was soon applied to all types of three- and four-wheeled carriages to make "cars" of all kinds. By 1896 the high-speed gasoline engine was tried out on a wagon by the Langert Company of Philadelphia, and the first "truck" was born!

No sooner had the first trucks taken to the roads than the first

*Bill Johnson and the first
moving van in California (1909).*

conflicts between the smokeys and the bandits began. Many local governments passed laws forbidding gasoline-powered trucks from using their streets and roads, because the vehicles frightened the horses and mules used by teamsters hauling freight in regular wagons. Just to be a driver of one of these newfangled trucks made one a "bandit" subject to being run off the streets or arrested for disturbing the peace.

Trucking became more respectable when a young graduate of Columbia Law School, A. L. Riker, built a battery-powered electric wagon for hauling freight. Riker's wagon and others like it were successful for a time, as was the quiet-running steam engine designed by the Stanley brothers of Newton, Massachusetts.

For a time it appeared that the outlawed "devil's wagon," as the gasoline-powered trucks were called, was doomed. In 1903, a 40-mile (64-km) race was run in New York City to see which type of self-propelled freight wagon was best. There were fourteen trucks made by eleven different truck-building companies entered in the race. The lightest truck was a steam-powered delivery wagon entered by the Mobile Company of America. It used gasoline instead of coal to fire its steam boiler and four and one-half horsepower to pull its 750-pound (340-kg) load. The heaviest truck was a giant machine called the Courtland, imported from England. It carried a load of 12,000 pounds (5,443 kg) powered by a thirty-horsepower coal-burning steam engine.

The winner of the contest turned out to be an eight-horsepower gasoline-powered truck called the Waterless Knox. With its air-cooled engine it made the 40-mile (64-km) round trip in three hours and thirty-five minutes using only 4 gallons (15 l) of gasoline. The big Courtland from England carried more weight by far but took much more time and consumed 890 pounds (403 kg) of coal and 115 gallons (435 l) of water! One of the electrics, a Waverly, made the trip in something over four hours and used only $2.50 worth of electricity.

Although the great truck race did not win public acceptance

for the gasoline-engine truck, it did prove that the steam-driven vehicles were not economically feasible. They had to make frequent stops to take on fuel and water, and that wasted the time of the driver, which was the most expensive part of transportation costs in those days. The electrics were economical, quiet, and efficient, but their thousands of pounds of batteries needed frequent recharging, so their range and payload was limited.

Then one summer, the gasoline-powered trucks and their drivers became heroes. On July 3, 1911, a heat wave hit New York City and 1,700 horses died of heat exhaustion on the streets in one day. Thousands more were disabled and became unable to perform their jobs of hauling freight. As the heat wave continued, thousands of gasoline-powered trucks came to the rescue, showing business people that they could deliver milk, meat, and vegetables while saving time and money.

Laws restricting the use of trucks began to be repealed and the "animal engine" (the horse) appeared doomed. The day of the dray horse finally ended during World War I.

Around 1918, America's primary transportation system, the railroads, began to break down. President Woodrow Wilson put the railroads under governmental control, but they still could not handle all the additional freight hauling made necessary by the war. Trucks began moving goods over routes that would not have been profitable before the war. Truck routes were established between many cities along the Atlantic seacoast. The army and navy began to use trucks to transport soldiers, sailors, and ammunition. Overseas trucks had proved themselves on the battlefield, and when the Great War was over the truck driver once again found himself a hero. He had brought food and ammunition to the troops and had carried the wounded off to field hospitals. Thousands of army trucks were left over and ready for private use. The returning war veterans brought their truck-driving skills back to their hometowns all across America.

Between the two world wars trucks and truckers made steady progress in the speed and dependability of their services. They

*In 1910 the Auto Delivery Company of Portland, Oregon,
could deliver the goods in both steam and gas trucks.*

*Between the two World Wars truckers
fought for better roads and bridges.*

fought for better bridges and roads; better, more dependable tires; and more comfort in the driver's seat for their long hauls. The truckers got what they wanted over the years. By 1940, such refinements as sleeper cabs had become popular on trucks designed for cross-country hauling.

Women Truckers and Husband-and-Wife Driving Teams

In the "old days" it took so much physical strength to drive and maintain a truck on the road that most women would not think of becoming truck drivers. Today, many women find the life of the truck driver on the open road attractive. Most say it is the travel and the freedom that they love most about their jobs. Many women drive trucks with their husbands. Most of these women learned truck driving from their husbands, relatives, or from farm experience. Some have graduated from truck-driving schools. While many women work alone on the road hauling every kind of load in every kind of truck, most are part of husband-and-wife truck-driving teams.

Living in the Truck Cab

The big rigs driven by husband-and-wife teams have all the comforts of home behind the driver's seat. A regular double-bed-sized sleeper also features a tiny electric kitchen for fixing coffee and snacks as well as a radio, stereo, and TV set. A small gasoline- or butane-driven electric power plant runs the air conditioner or heater and all the electrical equipment. A couple can spend a comfortable night in their truck and not waste any current in their truck battery or burn a drop of the diesel fuel that powers their truck.

Life on the Open Road

Life on the open road for truckers can be watching television in air-conditioned comfort in the middle of a desert, or feeling snug in back of the seat bunk with the cab heaters on when it's 20°F below zero (−29°C) outside. It's freedom and travel, being your own boss, and feeling close to other haulers sharing the road. It's having coffee and trading stories. But it can also be feeling scared and wondering if you'll make it alive through the next couple of days.

Doug Carry was both happy and worried about his new life as a trucker as he sat in the truck stop just south of St. Louis in the section marked "For Professional Drivers Only." Orm had gone to check the weather again. Doug listened to what some of the other truckers who had stopped there at Orm's request were saying about weather.

"I drove straight through a windstorm, a bunch of tornadoes, a sandstorm, and then a snowstorm one trip, one right after another, going from New Jersey to Arizona one time. The only thing that ever scares me is changes in the weather," one of the truckers commented.

"Wind is the worst thing," said another. "A real bad wind— say 55 miles (88 km) an hour blowing straight at your side—with an empty trailer can knock you off the road. There have been a few wrecks like that. The only good wind is a tail wind."

"I was driving the Interstate up through Arkansas," a trucker with "Jim" tattooed on his forearm said, "and I hit what they call 'black ice.' There is nothing more dangerous than that. The ice is so clear you don't see it. All you see is the blacktop. Anyway, I was moving right along in the fast lane on this crowded road. I came around a curve not knowing there was any ice on the road. When I tried to straighten out coming out of the curve I couldn't do it. I thought something had gone haywire with my steering. I was scared to death. I shut down my rig real easy and got out. The road was a sheet of ice. The wind had just slid me across the highway. I was so terrified I didn't drive any faster than 10 miles (16 km) an hour all the way to Little Rock."

Orm Stewart came back to report that the weather was getting worse, not better.

Hauling "double bottoms." When truck engines became
more powerful, truckers could pull heavier loads.

By 1940, sleeper cabs had become popular on trucks
designed for cross-country hauling. The new
streamlined designs helped increase gas mileage.

"Mother Nature is sure on a rampage out of Joplin," Orm told the group of truckers. "Wind, snow, sleet, ice, we're going to get it all. We'd best put our relief drivers on the pedal and get some shut-eye between here and Joplin and go on through to Texas tonight. If we wait 'til tomorrow we might not get through for several days."

OKLAHOMA ON ICE

Doug Carry drove the Mean Green Machine through Joplin, Missouri, and on across the border into Oklahoma. The Interstate stretched out wide and flat ahead and a few gentle flakes of snow drifted down from a dark sky. Doug knew there would be a lot more snow as they rolled deeper into the state toward the Texas border.

Orm was asleep in the big bunk behind the driver's seat. It would soon be time for Doug to wake him up and take a turn at getting some sleep. Doug wondered how he would ever be able to sleep with all the excitement ahead. He had been keeping in touch with the other truckers in their convoy on the CB radio. Doug knew the CB radio would be the most important factor in getting them safely through the night.

CB Radio

Doug remembered that he had first heard about trucks and trucking in 1974 when his dad had bought a CB radio for the family car.

The Arab oil embargo produced long lines at filling stations in December of 1973. President Richard Nixon asked the public to conserve as much gasoline and oil as possible. Truckers had to wait in long lines at fuel pumps and they saw the price of diesel fuel more than double in just a few weeks. Then Congress passed a law making it illegal to drive more than 55 miles (88 km) per hour on the nation's highways. All this increased the number of hours a trucker had to spend on the road with his load and cut down on their profits. It put some truckers out of business.

After appealing in vain to the federal government to get the "double nickel" speed limit eliminated and to lower fuel prices, the nation's truckers went on strike. They used their CB radios to coordinate truck movements and to organize protest convoys. Since it was a wildcat (illegal) strike, it was very exciting and was well covered by the news media. The colorful CB lingo caught on with the general public.

Many drivers other than truckers did not want to travel 55 miles (88 km) an hour on highways designed for speeds in excess of 75 miles (121 km) per hour, even to save fuel. So they bought CB radios for their "four-wheelers" and joined the truckers in their revolt against government authority, smokey.

Citizen band (CB) radio was first opened up to the general public in 1947, but the equipment was expensive, bulky, and not at all easy to operate. By the late 1950s, however, the government opened up new lower-frequency channels that gave the citizen band radios a wider range. The invention of the transistor had made the equipment small, portable, and easy to operate. And the Japanese electronics industry promoted their inexpensive CB radios to American truckers who found that the little short-range radios could save them time and money, keep them in touch with their families, and make the hours of solo driving less lonely. Until the fuel crisis in 1973–74, few people other than "ham" radio operators and truckers had even heard of CB radio.

When CB radio became popular, however, it was a landslide. In the twenty years prior to 1975, the Federal Communications Commission had issued just under one million licenses to CBers.

The next year, 1976, alone saw one million more issued. By the spring of 1977 more than ten million people were licensed to use CB radios to call for help when stranded on the highway, to inquire about road conditions, to report accidents quickly, and to issue and receive smokey reports.

CB radios now operate on any one of forty channels, with channel nine reserved for emergency calls only. It is monitored twenty-four hours a day, seven days a week, all across the country. No matter where you are, if you call for help on channel nine someone will hear you and respond.

It is very easy to get a license to operate a CB set. In fact, you usually get a license application form and a list of regulations when you buy a set. The license fee is very inexpensive. You must stay off channel nine except for emergencies. The only other official regulations are that you are supposed to give your call sign (which is printed on your license) every time you talk, or transmit, and you are supposed to wait for one minute after each five-minute transmission. To transmit, you simply pick up the mike and press a button. When you release the button you can hear anyone else who happens to be transmitting within range on the channel you are using.

The transmitting range of a CB set depends on the lay of the land. In flat country you can talk within a 10- to 15-mile (16- to- 24 km) range. In the city or in the mountains your range is often limited to about 3 miles (5 km). This is because the 27 MHz (megahertz) radio waves used in the CB band do not bend around objects like the lower-frequency AM broadcast band radio waves do. However, these 27 MHz radio waves do often bounce off of a layer of ionized air high up in the stratosphere and come back to earth hundreds of miles away from where they started. So CB radio sets are limited to not more than four watts of power, which is very low operating power. The bounced signal is so weak when it returns to earth that it is not picked up by the receiving end of a CB set.

Trucking Radio Stations

There are powerful radio stations on the AM broadcast band that specialize in late-night broadcasts beamed to truck drivers on the road. One of these stations, heard throughout the Midwest and Southwest, is WBAP in Fort Worth, Texas. All night long truckers can listen to their favorite country and western music, announcements of trucking events, reports on road conditions, and even messages to individual drivers and their families. Between the trucking radio stations and the CB radios in the tractors of most truckers, no one is ever out of touch with family, friends, or employers.

Hand and Light Signals

Even though truckers communicate quite a lot via radio, they often use hand and light signal communications to give messages to passing and oncoming trucks. This kind of signaling is quicker than using the radio and can be used while radio communication is going on with a third party. A trucker can also signal that a smokey is cruising the area without the risk of having smokey tune in. If a trucker wants to pass this message on, he or she flicks the headlights twice and holds up his or her first two fingers in a horizontal "V" formation.

When the weight stations are open this message can be passed along by raising one hand, palm up, or by giving the thumbs-up signal. Signaling with a closed fist indicates to another trucker that the weighing scales are closed down and the coast is clear. A wave of the logbook at another trucker signals that he or she is heading for a log check up ahead.

When a trucker rolls his or her hands around each other there is a wreck just up the road.

Light signals are used by truckers whether it is day or night. Many of these light signals are used just to be courteous to other truck and passenger car drivers. One blink of the headlights is a way of saying "Hello, how are you?" Two blinks is usually accompanied by a hand signal to indicate a speed trap, open weight station, or other legal check or inspection. Three blinks is always a signal to an oncoming truck or car that there is some kind of danger on the road ahead.

A trucker being passed signals by turning on his or her headlights when the passing truck gets a safe distance ahead. The signal tells the passing truck it is OK to pull back in the driving lane. The passing trucker blinks his marker lights once or twice to say "Thank you." Passenger car motorists—four-wheelers—often extend these signaling courtesies to truckers to make the highways friendlier and safer.

The High Cost of Delays

When trucks and their cargos get delayed it costs everybody money. In our society today the cost of transportation of goods sometimes represents a very large portion of the total cost of the goods. For example, a loaf of bread that sells for one dollar in the supermarket may contain only about eight-cents worth of ingredients. The rest of the cost represents profit and the cost of processing and transporting those ingredients. If shipments are delayed on the road for any reason, the consumer may have to pay the cost of that delay in the price of the commodity or service.

How Truckers' Decisions
Affect the Consumer

When Orm Stewart decided to take the Thompsons' furniture through the developing Oklahoma ice storm, rather than wait and risk having the highways shut down for several days, he made a decision that would determine when the Thompsons' would get their possessions and how much it would cost them. His decision could save them a lot of money and give them on-time delivery provided that he and Doug get through the stormy night without getting stranded or wrecking their rig. Whatever happened, the Thompsons would be favorably or adversely affected by the decisions their trucker made on the highway. Similarly, nearly all consumers of goods and services are affected for better or worse by the decisions that truckers have to make while pulling their loads across the country.

The Energy Crisis and
Its Effect on Trucking
Many of the decisions truckers make are related to the availability and price of fuel. The energy crisis that began with the Arab oil embargo in 1973 had a very profound effect on truckers. In fact, there was a steady decline in the number of independent truck owner-operators in the 1970s and early 1980s due to the fact that diesel fuel and gasoline for the big trucks climbed from around twenty-five cents a gallon to more than a dollar twenty-five cents a gallon. The big rigs can travel only 4 or 5 miles (6 or 8 km) on a gallon of gasoline or diesel fuel, so a trucker needs hundreds of dollars just to fill up his or her gas tank one time! You can see why the "money squeeze" put so many of them out of business. Those that stayed in business, of course, had to pass along this tremendous added cost to their customers, where it was added to the price of groceries, clothing, and many other consumer goods.

The Trucker and Courage
But most truckers handled the energy crisis and its money squeeze with their usual courage. For it takes courage indeed to study the principles of good business management and apply them in the face of possible failure. During the early 1980s, owner-operator truck drivers flocked to workshops and seminars offered by business schools and universities all over the country. They "hit the books" to learn better business practices that would keep them in business and earning enough money to live in a country where prices were constantly rising.

The Trucker as a
Hard-Working Professional
It not only takes courage but long hours of hard work to keep up with the latest money-saving business practices, state and federal

regulations and deregulations, new equipment, instrumentation, engines, fuel mixtures, maintenance procedures—and the weather.

Doug Carry was thinking about all the things he had to learn and do to be a good professional trucker. Suddenly he felt control of the big moving rig slipping away from him. There was a jerk on the tractor and Doug's heart started to pound as he felt the trailer jerk the other way. He looked into his rearview mirror and saw the running light of the trailer coming up at him sideways!

Orm Stewart had awakened and sat up in the bunk. "It's that old devil black ice," Orm said calmly as he squinted out the windshield at the snow swirling over the dark highway. Then he saw their trailer coming at them in the rearview mirror.

"Just tap the brakes really lightly to straighten out that jack-knife," he told Doug, "and then shut the rig down real easy. Easy does it."

●●●●●●●● 4

HOME FREE

Doug Carry used everything he had ever learned about handling a big rig on ice. His heart was racing and he was scared to death, but he did it all slow and easy, just like Orm said. He couldn't keep the big moving van on the highway, but he did keep the rig and its valuable cargo all in one piece. After what seemed like hours, but was actually only a minute or two, Doug had the rig under control and rolling very slowly down the median strip of the Interstate. Orm was already on the CB radio warning the trucks that were following them about the invisible ice that was now forming on the highway.

The Mean Green Machine was the "front door" of the convoy, which means that all the others were following close behind, and all were traveling at the same speed.

Orm had suggested that the whole convoy slow down for a while, not just because of the ice but because the snow was now heavier and mixed with sleet that beat ominously on the hood and windshield.

"You handled that emergency like a veteran," Orm told Doug. "I didn't think you were such a cool character!"

"Thanks Orm," Doug replied, "but I didn't feel cool at all. I was plenty scared."

"To tell you the truth, so was I," Orm said. "Anyway, you've earned your turn on the bunk. I'll take the Machine on down to Texas."

Sleeping was the last thing that Doug felt like doing, but he knew he had to get some rest to be fresh for driving the next day, since they were going straight through. Actually, the driving conditions were not too bad. They just had to get through before conditions got worse.

Handling Disasters and Emergencies

Back in the bunk, Doug couldn't help thinking about what might have happened if he had not been able to bring that dangerous jackknifing skid under control. What if he had been on a bridge and there had been no handy median strip to slide into and maneuver in?

Most truckers feel that they can handle any disaster or emergency, but that the best bet is to avoid trouble by keeping their rigs in good shape. That way almost all accidents and breakdowns can be avoided. During winter on a cross-country run, drivers try to get through before conditions get too bad for safe driving. When that happens they have to shut down their rigs and wait it out. To try to drive through blizzards and severe winter storms is to invite trouble.

Fire is not a common occurrence, but when it happens most truckers just get out of their trucks and out of the way. They do carry fire extinguishers, but they know that their little 1¾-pound (.8-kg) extinguishers can't be used to fight 200 or more gallons (757 l) of exploding, burning diesel fuel.

You might think that loosing a wheel or blowing a tire would be an emergency situation for a trucker. Actually, the drivers *behind* the truck will know about a blown tire before the truck driver will. Sometimes truck tires spew rubber all over the road when they blow, while at other times they just bubble up and go flat. The rig has so many wheels and such stiff suspension that the trucker may not become aware of this problem until he or she makes the next stop.

• 36

Sometimes a truck looses an entire wheel. There is not much a driver can do about that while traveling at high speed. It won't greatly affect the way the truck handles, but it can be quite a hazard to any four-wheeler that might be following. If the lost wheel happens to be one of the two front wheels on the steering axle, it can be disastrous. But that type of accident doesn't happen if the trucker keeps his or her rig in good condition and checks it often.

One of the worst hazards a trucker must face is bad roads. Stretches of road that aren't kept in first-class condition have sometimes wrecked trucks in spite of everything a driver does. Again, this type of disaster can best be handled by avoiding it in the first place. Drivers keep in touch by radio and during meal stops, informing each other about dangerous road conditions.

Night driving, even in good weather, presents another kind of potential danger. Drivers have to be able to see and be seen by other drivers. That is why truckers make certain they have a lot of running lights—the kind that are all over the tractor and trailers. A lot of truckers use powerful quartz fog or driving lights. But even with strong driving lights, if a truck is the only vehicle on the road the driver can't see very far ahead. If there *is* traffic they often use what they call the "guinea pig" method. That is, they always drive behind someone else's taillights. Those taillights out in front tell a great deal about what is happening on the road ahead. When the other driver's brake lights suddenly go on, it's a signal that something is happening up ahead. With the guinea pig method, however, the trucker must hope that the driver ahead has lights that are working properly.

How Public Safety Officers and Truckers Cooperate

Public safety officers and truckers do play their game of "smokey and bandit," but the state public safety police officer is the trucker's "good buddy" when it comes to keeping the roads safe and offering quick help in an emergency. Almost all officers monitor CB channel nine, the emergency channel, while cruising in their patrol cars, and they respond quickly to any distress call from a trucker. They are also ready to administer first aid and get an injured trucker to a nearby hospital the quickest way possible. Sometimes in the western states this means calling in the state's public safety helicopter. Even the enforcement of speed limits, the inspection of truckers' logbooks, and checks on permits are ways of making the roads safer and faster for all truckers. Cooperation with public safety officers is another way professional truckers stay out of trouble and get their load delivered safely and on time.

Convoy and Cooperation Win the Battle

Most truckers agree that if there is any one word to describe success in the trucking business it is "cooperation." Cooperation made possible the convoy Orm Stewart organized to get himself and a group of his fellow truckers through Oklahoma before the roads turned to ice. Just that one spot of black ice that gave Doug such a scare might have wrecked one or more of the other trucks had they not been traveling in a convoy and keeping in touch by CB radio.

All night long the convoy rolled slowly through the developing ice storm, avoiding mishaps by keeping one another informed. They all kept their AM radios tuned to WBAP in Fort Worth, Texas, one of the powerful truckers' radio stations that broadcast the latest weather reports and road conditions. And they cooperated with the public safety officers to keep the Interstate safe for other travelers.

Doug Carry never thought he could sleep through it all, so when he found himself being awakened at a truck stop he couldn't believe it.

"We've made Big D, old buddy," Orm was saying to him. "No more ice and snow. We won the battle. Come on. All we need now is a Texas-sized breakfast!"

•••••••5
TRUCKING SHOW

"Welcome to Alamo Town," Orm said to Doug later that afternoon as they topped a hill on Interstate 35 and the skyline of San Antonio, Texas, suddenly appeared before them.

"Wow, its bigger than I thought," exclaimed Doug.

"Bigger than I ever thought it would get to be," replied Orm, "and big enough for that big trucking show you wanted to see."

"Since we drove through the night last night and put ourselves nearly a day ahead of schedule, maybe we just ought to give ourselves a treat and take it all in," Doug said.

"Can't deliver that furniture until in the morning anyway," said Orm with a wink. "So I'll say ten-four to that, good buddy!"

Orm and Doug parked their rig at a big truck stop, showered, shaved, and caught a ride to San Antonio's big convention center on Hemisphere Plaza. Doug was really anxious to see the new tractors on display at the trucking show, because his ambition was to own one for himself and become an independent owner-operator.

Today's Trucks
Doug had been advised by other truckers that he would have to have a good tractor—the newer the better—to get into business.

Lots of hauling companies require that their truckers' tractors be less than five years old.

Tractors haven't changed much mechanically over the years. What has changed are the features that make the truck driver more comfortable. And that's the main thing a trucker looks for when he is in the market for a new tractor. All of today's truck manufacturers have their stories to tell to prospective truck owners about their own individual "packages" for driver comfort. Kenworth and Peterbilt are major truck manufacturers. Some truckers say that Freightliner, another well-known manufacturer, produces easy-riding trucks that, once broken in, run hundreds of thousands of miles with no trouble. The cabs are loaded with enough gauges and controls to make one feel like the captain of a spaceship. They, like most other trucks, come with a small auxiliary gasoline- or butane-driven electric plant to run the television, radios, and air conditioning. A trucker can sit in comfort in the middle of the desert and watch television without using a drop of diesel fuel!

Peterbilt tractors are all hand built. The company builds only five or six a day and some truckers say they will outlast anything on the road. Petes have luxury sleeping compartments, if that's what the trucker wants, with wide double bunks and a mini-kitchen for brewing coffee and fixing snacks.

Kenworth makes a double-decked sleeper cab that looks like a spaceship coming down the road. On top of the normal sleeper is a second deck with its own windshield that puts the sleeping bunk high up and offers a view of the road ahead. Kenworth cabs are roomy and good for two-person driving teams.

There are a lot of other companies that build fine, roomy, comfortable trucks in styles that feature the engine in front of the cab (conventionals) or underneath the cab (cabovers). Some of the other brand names you will find on the road are Dodge, Ford, General Motors (GM), International, Mack, and Mercedes-Benz.

There are all kinds of extras that truckers can put on their trucks. These include a "headache rack" (to keep the load from banging against the back of the cab), air suspension (for a smoother ride), and an engine turbocharger (for more speed and power). Then there are the radios: CB, AM, FM; stereo tape players; TV sets; coffee makers—all devices to make the driver feel at home. After all, most long-haul truckers spend twenty-two to twenty-four days a month living in their trucks.

It takes about as much money to buy and equip a tractor-trailer rig as it does to buy a house in the suburbs. But truckers usually pay for their trucks as they use them over a five-year period. A lot of truckers buy reconditioned used trucks which cost a lot less money.

Tomorrow's Trucks

Now that trucks have been made as comfortable as possible to drive and live in, what do the designers have in mind for tomorrow's trucks? What kind of trucks will truckers be using to haul their loads in the 1990s and the year 2001?

There is one type of eighteen-wheeler already on the roads today that has been called by some the truck of the future. It is the new Ruan Mega million-miler. It is said to be able to run for 1 million miles (1.6 million km) without the need for a major overhaul, eliminating much expensive maintenance and downtime for the truck owners. Until the Ruan Mega, most trucks could not run even a *half* a million miles without a major overhaul.

According to what is on the drawing boards today, tomorrow's trucks will use fuel much more efficiently, getting many more miles to the gallon of diesel fuel than today's trucks. In fact, many of the new designs call for steam-powered truck engines that can run on a wide range of fuels such as liquified coal, hydrogen, and even wood chips. There will be more safety features on trucks of the future. Trailers may even be replaced by trucks made out of one piece of flexible material that will bend around curves! This will enable designers to relocate the cab in relation to the load, so that the load can serve to protect drivers from bad crashes.

One of the best features of the trucks coming around the turn of the century will be the use of on-board computers that will not only keep drivers informed about the condition of their engines and loads, but that will help them with their business matters. These business "brains" will take into consideration the many variables that truckers can't possibly keep track of and advise them what routes to take and what speeds to travel at in order to make the most profit from the trip. If a trucker is running behind in his or her logbook, the computer can bring it right up to the minute in less time than it will take a smokey to flag him or her down.

Already, computers installed in the highway at some weight station locations are weighing trucks as they move at top speed down the highway so that truckers never even have to slow down unless they are over the legal weight limit!

How to Become a Trucker

Companies that sell new tractors and trailers will give someone who wants to get started in the trucking business all the help they need, even if the person has never been in the cab of a truck before. They will sell him or her the truck and accessories, arrange to have the whole "package" financed, and get him or her a job or hauling contract with one of the many firms that are willing to employ inexperienced people just starting out. The only requirement is that the person have a good driving record for two years before they start trucking. If a person has a bad record of driving a four-wheeler and a lot of speeding tickets, no one will even sell him a truck, much less entrust their cargo to such a driver. As one of the truck salesmen at the trucking show said to Doug and Orm, "The insurance rates are the big thing nowadays. If the guy or gal has a clean driving record, we can sell him a truck, get him a license, sell him on a job, and put him or her to work."

Trucking Schools

Not all dealers are willing to do so much for their customers. Even if the customer does have a perfect driving record, the best idea is to take a trucking job and save for a down payment. That way, too,

A trucker needs a good tractor—the newer the better—to get into business.

one can get a better idea of what one wants to haul and what kind of truck is needed.

While many trucking companies have their own driver-training programs, a lot of young men and women learn the ropes by going to one of the many truck-driving schools around the country. Insurance companies encourage this and often offer lower rates to new drivers who are graduates of truck-driving schools. These schools teach how to drive and back tractor-trailer rigs. Some schools help students pass the driving-license examinations and set up the books and records a truck driver must keep.

Meanwhile, truckers are telling young people to learn all they can about trucks and the geography of their country. All agree that students need to concentrate on math, reading, and writing skills if they hope to become successful truckers. More information on becoming a trucker is available at the library. Consult the *Occupational Outlook Handbook* published by the U.S. Department of Labor.

What Trucking Offers
Both Men and Women

A lot of women truckers have been taught to drive and taught the trucking business by their husbands. One young woman having coffee with Doug and Orm told them, "My husband taught me driving—the whole business. When I got my first job I didn't know how to back a rig up and I told them I didn't. They just said, 'Can you stay out of ditches?' I said, 'That I can do.' They said, 'You've got the job.'"

Both she and her husband agreed that they were truckers because they loved to be out traveling on the open road. They made good money, but better still was their feeling about how important trucking is to their country. Without the eighteen-wheelers and their loads the whole country would be in trouble.

Delivering the Goods

When Doug and Orm delivered the Thompsons' household goods to them the next morning at their new address in San Antonio,

Texas, Mr. Thompson was very surprised to see them arriving on time.

"We heard on the news last night that all the roads through Oklahoma were closed because of a terrible ice and snow storm," Mr. Thompson told them. "We were worried about our belongings."

"Well, we were in just about the last convoy to get through early yesterday morning before the weather closed in," Orm said modestly.

While Orm finalized the business arrangements with Mr. Thompson, Doug helped with the unloading. Mrs. Thompson unpacked her expensive china, delighted that not a piece was broken. Doug thought about black ice and whirling snow on a dark highway and how he had had to use all his skill and courage to get the truck under control again. He remembered that Orm had said, "I didn't think you were such a cool character," and he felt every bit as tall as the Mean Green Machine, which was just exactly 13 feet (4 m).

GLOSSARY

Advertising sign—a marked police car with lights and siren on.

Air bear or Astronaut—police in helicopter or airplane.

Back door—last truck in a convoy.

Bear—police officer.

Bear report—report on police locations.

Bear trap—radar in operation.

Big 10-4—acknowledgement with enthusiasm.

Black ice—an almost invisible patch of ice on an otherwise clear road.

Bobtail—a truck tractor without a trailer, or a two-axle straight truck.

Boon dockin'—avoiding weight stations by taking back roads or otherwise running illegally.

Break or Breaker—Request for permission to use CB channel. ("Breaker one-nine," means "I want to talk on channel nineteen.")

Bull hauler—a livestock hauler.

Cabover—a truck with the cab sitting over the engine. Also called a "flatface."

Cherry picker—an extra-high cabover tractor.

Chicken coop—weight station.

Chicken inspector—person in charge at the weight station.

Clearance lights—the amber lights mounted on either side of a tractor's roof. On trailers these lights are red and mounted on both sides, front, rear, and center.

Common carrier—a trucker or trucking company that offers freight service to the general public rather than exclusively to one company.

Cummins—a large manufacturer of diesel engines.

Cylinder—that part of the engine block that houses the pistons.

Deadhead—running a truck without a load. Also called "hauling postholes," "sailboat fuel," "Volkswagen radiators"—anything that is "nothing."

Deep under—lowest gear ratio in the transmission.

Detroit Diesel—a GMC diesel engine.

Doghouse—an engine located inside the cab. Also may refer to a sleeping compartment behind the cab.

Double clutch—depressing the clutch twice when shifting; once when taking the truck out of gear and again when putting it into the new gear. This allows the trucker to change the speed of his engine while in neutral in order to make a smoother shift.

Double nickel—55 miles (88 km) per hour.

Doughnuts—truck tires.

Dragon wagon—a wrecker.

Drop the hammer—accelerate.

Ears on—CB radio turned on.

Eighteen-wheeler—any tractor-trailer rig regardless of the number of wheels it actually has.

ETA—estimated time of arrival.

Eyeball—face-to-face meeting, or look.

Fifth wheel—a large steel disc on the back of a tractor used to couple the tractor to its trailer. It locks with a kingpin. When a truck is out of control because the trailer is swaying, it is said to be "driven by the fifth wheel," a dangerous situation.

Flatbed—a trailer without sides or top.

Floating the gears—shifting without using the clutch.

Foxy lady—attractive woman.

Four-wheeler—automobile.

Front door—first vehicle in a convoy.

Full trailer—a trailer with wheels on both ends. A trailer with wheels on only one end is a "semi-trailer."

Fuzzbuster—radar detecting device.

Gear jammer—a truck driver.

Glow plug—a device that heats up the engine and the fuel, making a truck engine easier to start.

Go breaker—permission granted to talk on a CB channel.

Good buddy—any other CBer.

Good numbers—best wisher.

Got a copy?—did anybody hear me?

Governor—a device that limits engine speed by controlling the amount of fuel that reaches the engine.

Green stamps—speeding tickets or money.

Gypsy—an independent trucker. An owner-operator who will haul anything, anywhere, for anybody.

Hammer—accelerator.

Handle—CB nickname.

Hot load—a rush shipment.

Hundred-mile coffee—strong coffee. (It'll keep one going another hundred miles.)

ICC—Interstate Commerce Commission. A government agency that regulates trucking and other businesses that do business in more than one state.

ID lights—identification lights mounted three together on top of the tractor and on the rear of the trailer.

Jackknife—trailer skids and swings around on the fifth wheel toward the tractor. The trailer can actually collide with the tractor if the jackknife is not brought under control, a very difficult maneuver.

Kidney buster—a truck with a rough ride.

Logbook—a written record of the driver's trips and the time spent on and off duty. Sometimes called "comic books." Drivers can be fined if their logbooks are not kept up-to-date.

Lowboy—a trailer made for hauling heavy equipment.

Marker lights—same as clearance lights.

Mayday—"I am in distress."

Mile marker—mile posts along the highway.

Over—transmission completed, but still listening.

Over shoulder—behind.

Pair of sevens—no contact.

Pete or Petercar—nickname for a Peterbilt truck.

Piggyback—transportation of trailers on a railroad flatcar.

Pin-up—the hooking up of a tractor to a trailer.

Put on the air—apply the brakes.

Put on the irons—put on snow chains.

Radio check—check on the quality and strength of a CB signal.

Read—hear.

Reefer—a refrigerated trailer.

Rig—a tractor-trailer combination, a truck.

Rocking chair—middle vehicle in a convoy.

Roger—I acknowledge.

Saddle tanks—fuel tanks mounted on the side of the truck, below or behind the cab.

Semi-trailer—a trailer with wheels only on the rear end. The other end is equipped to couple to the fifth wheel of a tractor.

Shanty shaker—a trucker who hauls mobile homes.

Sick horse—a tractor in need of repair, or a trucker moving slower than the rest of the traffic on the road.

Six-wheeler—automobile pulling a trailer.

Slam bang—dump truck.

Smile and comb your hair—CBer's warning that there is radar monitoring on the road ahead.

Smokey—a police officer.

Split shift—shifting two transmissions at once as when the transmission is upshifted and the rear axle is downshifted.

Squealer—a tachograph. (See below.)

Squelch—an electronic circuit in a receiving set that shuts off the speaker unless a strong signal is coming in. It cuts out background noise.

Tachograph—a device that automatically records the number of miles a truck is driven, its speed, the hours driven, and the number of stops made.

Tandem axles—two axles set one behind the other.

Ten-code—abbreviated form of conversation, first used by police and now widely used by truckers. (See next page, "How to Break the Ten-Code.")

Turbocharger—a supercharger (forced-air carburation) driven by exhaust gases.

Two-wheeler—motorcycle.

Uncle Charlie—The Federal Communications Commission (FCC).

Water hole—truck stop.

Wilco—"I will comply."

Window washer—rainstorm.

Wrapper—color of a car. A blue wrapper is a blue car. Usually used to refer to unmarked police cars.

XYL—wife.

XYM—husband.

YL—young lady.

YM—young man.

Zoo—police station.

HOW TO BREAK THE TEN-CODE

The unofficial CB ten-code listed here is derived from, but not identical to, the official ten-code used by law enforcement agencies. Where there are missing numbers there is simply no CB ten-code that is used. For example, in the law enforcement code, 10-14 is a prowler report and 10-15 is a civil disturbance. The CB code has no equivalent numbers.

10-1	Receiving poorly
10-2	Receiving well
10-3	Stop transmitting
10-4	Okay, acknowledged
10-5	Relay message
10-6	Busy, stand by
10-7	Out of service
10-8	In service
10-9	Repeat message
10-10	Transmission completed, standing by
10-11	Talking too rapidly
10-12	Visitors present
10-13	Advise weather and road conditions

10–16	Make pickup at_____
10–17	Urgent business
10–18	Anything for us?
10–19	Nothing for you, return to base
10–20	Location
10–21	Call by telephone
10–22	Report in person to_____
10–23	Stand by
10–24	Assignment completed
10–25	Can you contact?
10–26	Disregard last information
10–27	Moving to channel_____
10–28	Identify your station
10–29	Leaving this location, time is up for contact
10–30	Does not conform to FCC rules
10–31	Crime in progress
10–32	Radio check
10–33	Emergency traffic, this station
10–34	Trouble here, need help
10–35	Confidential information
10–36	Correct time
10–39	Your message delivered
10–44	I have a message for_____
10–45	All units please report
10–46	Assist motorist
10–50	Break channel
10–51	Wrecker needed
10–52	Ambulance needed
10–53	Road blocked
10–59	Convoy or escort
10–60	What is next message number?
10–62	Unable to copy, use phone
10–63	Prepare to make written copy
10–64	Not directed to
10–65	Not clear

10–66	Message cancellation
10–67	All units comply
10–68	Repeat message
10–69	Have you dispatched message?
10–70	Fire at_____
10–73	Speed trap at_____
10–75	You are causing interference
10–77	ETA. (Estimated Time of Arrival)
10–82	Reserve room or lodging
10–84	My telephone number is _____
10–85	My address is_____
10–88	Advise telephone number of_____
10–89	Radio repairman needed
10–91	Talk closer to mike
10–92	Have your transmitter checked
10–93	Check my frequency
10–94	Give me a long count
10–95	Test with no modulation
10–99	Mission completed
10–100	Personal reasons
10–200	Police needed at _____

LIST OF TRUCKING AM RADIO STATIONS

KBOI
Boise, Idaho   670

KGA
Spokane, Washington   1510

KLAC
Los Angeles, California   570

KOB
Albuquerque, New Mexico   770

KPNW
Eugene, Oregon   1120

KVOO
Tulsa, Oklahoma   1170

WBAP
Fort Worth, Texas   820

WLW
Cincinnati, Ohio   700

WMAQ
Chicago, Illinois   670

WRVA
Richmond, Virginia   1140

WWVA
Wheeling, West Virginia   1170

Broadcasts directly to truck drivers usually take place from midnight to dawn.

FOR FURTHER READING

Donnelly, Warren. *Traveling with a Radio*. Colorado Springs: Donnelly & Sons Publishing Company, 1979

Goldberg, Naomi & Lesberg, Steve. *Hammer Down*. New York: Peebles Press, 1977

Lynot, John. *Loaded and Rollin'*. New York: Charles Scribner's Sons, 1979

Robinson, John. *Highways and Our Environment*. New York: McGraw-Hill Book Company, 1971

Russell, P.J. *The Motor Wagons*. Akron: The Pioneer Motor Traffic Club of Akron, 1971

Stern, Jane. *Trucker: A Portrait of the Last American Cowboy*. New York: McGraw-Hill Book Company, 1975

Thomas, James H. *The Long Haul*. Memphis: Memphis State University Press, 1979

INDEX